My Seasons

Siobhan Dodds

W

FRANKLIN WATTS

LONDON • SYDNEY

In spring we like

hiding and peeping,

jumping

and skipping.

In summer we like

digging and bouncing,

running and swimming.

In autumn we like

collecting and crawling,

walking and climbing.

In winter we like

rolling and waving,

building and sliding.

What am I doing?

What are we building?

What am I using to
dig the sand?

What is our puppy doing in the snow?

What's fun to do when it's hot?

 What do we wear in the cold?

Sharing books with your child

Early Worms are a range of books for you to share with your child. Together you can look at the pictures and talk about the subject or story. Listening, looking and talking are the first vital stages in children's reading development, and lay the early foundation for good reading habits.

Talking about the pictures is the first step in involving children in the pages of a book, especially if the subject or story can be related to their own familiar world. When children can relate the matter in the book to their own experience, this can be used as a starting point for introducing new knowledge, whether it is counting, getting to know colours or finding out how other people live.

Gradually children will develop their listening and concentration skills as well as a sense of what a book is. Soon they will learn how a book works: that you turn the pages from right to left, and read the story from left to right on a double page. They start to realize that the black marks on the page have a meaning and that they relate to the pictures. Once children have grasped these basic essentials they will develop strategies for "decoding" the text such as matching words and pictures, and recognising the rhythm of the language in order to predict what comes next. Soon they will start to take on the role of an independent reader, handling and looking at books even if they can't yet read the words.

Most important of all, children should realize that books are a source of pleasure. This stems from your reading sessions which are times of mutual enjoyment and shared experience. It is then that children find the key to becoming real readers.

This edition first published in 2002

Franklin Watts
96 Leonard Street
London EC2A 4XD

Franklin Watts Australia
45-51 Huntley Street
Alexandria
NSW 2015

ISBN 0 7496 4678 0

A CIP catalogue record for this book is available from the British Library

First published as *My Seasons* in the Early Worms series

Printed in Belgium

Consultants: Sue Robson and Alison Kelly,
Senior Lecturers in Education,
Faculty of Education, Early Childhood Centre,
Roehampton Institute, London

Sleeping Beauty

and other stories

Miles
KeLLy

First published in 2011 by Miles Kelly Publishing Ltd
Harding's Barn, Bardfield End Green, Thaxted, Essex, CM6 3PX, UK

Copyright © Miles Kelly Publishing Ltd 2011

2 4 6 8 10 9 7 5 3 1

Publishing Di *her*

Reprographics ne King, Jennifer Hunt

ISBN 978-1-84810-504-1

Printed in China

British Library Cataloguing-in-Publication Data
A catalogue record for this book is available from the British Library

ACKNOWLEDGEMENTS
Artworks are from the Miles Kelly Artwork Bank

Cover artwork by Frank Endersby (Beehive Illustration)

Every effort has been made to acknowledge the source and copyright holder of each picture.
Miles Kelly Publishing apologises for any unintentional errors or omissions.

Made with paper from a sustainable forest
www.mileskelly.net
info@mileskelly.net
www.factsforprojects.com

Contents

The Saviours of the Train

From *The Railway Children* by E Nesbit

*T*HE RUSSIAN gentleman was so delighted with the strawberries that the three racked their brains to find some other surprise for him. But all the racking did not bring out any idea more novel than wild cherries.

The cherry trees were some way from Three Chimneys, so Mother let them take their lunch with them in a basket. And the basket would do to bring the cherries back in if they found any. She also lent them her silver watch so that they should not be late for tea.

Near the tunnel was a flight of steps leading down to the line – just wooden bars roughly fixed into the earth – a very steep and narrow way.

"We'd better get down," said Peter; "I'm sure the cherries would be quite easy to get at from the side of the steps. You remember it was there we picked the cherry blossoms that we put on the rabbit's grave."

So they went along the fence towards the little swing gate that is at the top of these steps. And they were almost at the gate when Bobbie said: –

"Hush. Stop! What's that?"

'That' was a very odd noise – it was a sort of

rustling, whispering sound. As they listened it stopped, and then it began again. And this time it did not stop, but it grew louder and more rustling and rumbling.

"Look," cried Peter "the tree over there!"

And, as Peter pointed, the tree was moving – not just the way trees ought to move when the wind blows, but all in one piece, as though it were a live creature and were walking down the side of the cutting.

"It's moving!" cried Bobbie.

"It's magic," said Phyllis, breathlessly. "I always knew this railway was enchanted. What is it? It's much too magic for me. I don't like it. Let's go home."

But Bobbie and Peter clung fast to the rail and watched breathlessly. And Phyllis made no movement towards going home by herself.

The trees moved on and on. Some stones and loose earth fell and rattled on the railway metals below.

"It's ALL coming down," Peter tried to say, but he found there was hardly any voice to say it with. And, indeed, just as he spoke, the great rock, on the top of which the walking trees were, leaned slowly forward. The trees, ceasing to walk, stood still and shivered. Leaning with the rock, they seemed to hesitate a moment, and then rock and trees and grass and bushes, with a rushing sound, slipped right away from the face of the cutting and fell on the line with a blundering crash that could have been heard half a mile off. A cloud of dust rose up.

"Oh," said Peter, in awestruck tones, "isn't it exactly like when coals come in? – if there wasn't any roof to the cellar and you could see down."

"Look what a great mound it's made!" said Bobbie.

"Yes," said Peter, slowly. He was still leaning on the fence. Then he stood upright.

"The 11.29 down hasn't gone by yet. We must let them know at the station, or there'll be a most frightful accident."

"Let's run," said Bobbie, and began.

But Peter cried, "Come back!" and looked at Mother's watch. He was very prompt and businesslike, and his face looked whiter than they had ever seen it.

"No time," he said; "it's two miles away, and it's past eleven."

"Couldn't we climb up a telegraph post and do something to the wires?" suggested Phyllis.

"We don't know how," said Peter.

"They do it in war," said Phyllis; "I've heard of it."

"They only CUT them, silly," said Peter, "and that doesn't do any good. And we couldn't cut them even if we got up, and we couldn't get up. If we had some cloth, we could get down on the line and wave it."

"But the train wouldn't see us till it got round the corner, and then it could see the mound just as well as us," said Phyllis.

"If we only had some cloth," Peter repeated, "we could go round the corner and wave to the train."

"We might wave, anyway."

"They'd only think it was just US, as usual. We've waved so often before. Anyway, let's get down."

They got down the steep stairs. Bobbie was pale and shivering. Peter's face looked thinner than usual. Phyllis was red-faced and damp with anxiety.

"Oh, how hot I am!" she said; "and I thought it was going to be cold; I wish we hadn't put on our – " she stopped short, and then ended in quite a different tone – "our flannel petticoats."

Bobbie turned at the bottom of the stairs.

"Oh, yes," she cried; "Let's take them off."

They did, and with the petticoats rolled up under their arms, ran along the railway. They reached the corner that hid the mound from the straight line of railway that ran half a mile without curve or corner.

"Now," said Peter, taking hold of the largest petticoat.

"You're not" – Phyllis faltered – "you're not going to TEAR them?"

"Shut up," said Peter, with brief sternness.

"Oh, yes," said Bobbie, "tear them into little bits if you like. Don't you see, Phil, if we can't stop the train, there'll be a real live accident, with people KILLED. Oh, horrible! Here, Peter, you'll never tear it through the band!"

She took the flannel petticoat from him and tore it off an inch from the band. Then she tore the other in the same way.

"There!" said Peter, tearing in his turn. He divided each petticoat into three pieces. "Now, we've got six flags." He looked at the watch again. "And we've got seven minutes. We must have flagstaffs."

The knives given to boys are, for some odd reason, seldom of the kind of steel that keeps sharp. The young saplings had to be broken off. Two came up by the roots. The leaves were stripped from them.

"We must cut holes in the flags, and run the sticks through the holes," said Peter. And the holes were cut. The knife was sharp enough to cut flannel with. Two of the flags were set up in heaps of loose stones between the sleepers of the down line. Then Phyllis and Roberta took each a flag, and stood ready to wave it as soon as the train came in sight.

"I shall have the other two myself," said Peter, "because it was my idea to wave something."

"They're our petticoats, though," Phyllis was beginning, but Bobbie interrupted –

"Oh, what does it matter who waves what, if we can only save the train?"

Perhaps Peter had not rightly calculated the number of minutes it would take the 11.29 to get from the station to the place where they were, or perhaps the train was late. Anyway, it seemed a very long time that they waited.

It seemed to her that they had been standing there for hours and hours, holding those silly little flannel flags that no one would ever notice. The train wouldn't care. It would go rushing by them and tear round the corner and go crashing into that awful mound. And everyone would be killed. And then came the distant rumble and hum of the metals, and a puff of white steam showed far away along the stretch of line.

"Stand firm," said Peter, "and wave like mad! When it gets to that big furze bush step back, but go on waving! Don't stand ON the line, Bobbie!"

The train came rattling along very, very fast.

"They don't see us! They won't see us! It's all no good!" cried Bobbie.

The two little flags on the line swayed as the nearing train shook and loosened the heaps of loose stones that held them up. One of them slowly leaned over and fell on the line. Bobbie jumped forward and caught it up, and waved it; her hands did not tremble now.

It seemed that the train came on as fast as ever. It was very near now.

"Keep off the line, you silly cuckoo!" said Peter.

"It's no good," Bobbie said again.

"Stand back!" cried Peter, suddenly, and he dragged Phyllis back by the arm.

But Bobbie cried, "Not yet, not yet!" and waved her two flags right over the line. The front of the engine looked black and enormous.

"Oh, stop, stop, stop!" cried Bobbie. No one heard her. At least Peter and Phyllis didn't, for the oncoming rush of the train covered the sound of her voice with a mountain of sound. But afterwards she used to wonder whether the engine itself had not heard her, for it slackened swiftly, slackened and stopped, not twenty yards from the place where Bobbie's two flags waved over the line. She saw the great black engine stop dead, but somehow she could not stop waving the flags. And when the driver and the fireman had got off the engine and Peter and Phyllis had gone to meet them and pour out their excited tale of the awful mound just round the corner, Bobbie still waved the flags.

When the others turned towards her she was lying across the line with her hands flung forward and still gripping the sticks of the little flannel flags.

The engine-driver picked her up, carried her to the train, and laid her on the cushions.

"Gone right off in a faint," he said, "poor little woman. And no wonder. I'll just 'ave a look at this 'ere mound of yours, and then we'll run you back to the station and get her seen to."

It was horrible to see Bobbie lying so white and quiet, with her lips blue, and parted.

They sat by Bobbie on the blue cushions, and the train ran back. Before it reached their station Bobbie had sighed and opened her eyes, and rolled herself over and begun to cry. This cheered the others wonderfully. They had seen her cry before, but they had never seen her faint. They had not known what to do when she was fainting, but now she was only crying they could thump her on the back and tell her not to, just as they always did. And presently, when she stopped crying, they were able to laugh at her for being such a coward as to faint.

When the station was reached, the three were the heroes of an agitated meeting on the platform.

The praises they got for their "prompt action," their

"common sense," their "ingenuity," were enough to have turned anybody's head. Phyllis enjoyed herself thoroughly. She had never been a real heroine before, and the feeling was delicious. Peter's ears got very red. Yet he, too, enjoyed himself. Only Bobbie wished they all wouldn't. She wanted to get away.

"You'll hear from the Company about this, I expect," said the Station Master.

Bobbie wished she might never hear of it again. She pulled at Peter's jacket.

"Oh, come away! I want to go home," she said.

So they went. And as they went, everyone sent up a cheer.

"Oh, listen," cried Phyllis; "that's for US!"

"Yes," said Peter. "I say, I am glad I thought about waving something."

"How lucky WE put on our flannel petticoats!" said Phyllis.

Bobbie said nothing. She was thinking of the horrible mound, and the train rushing towards it.

"And it was US that saved them," said Peter.

"How dreadful if they had all been killed!" said Phyllis; "wouldn't it, Bobbie?"

"We never got any cherries, after all," said Bobbie.

The others thought her rather heartless.

The White Cat

By E Nesbit

THE WHITE CAT lived at the back of a shelf at the darkest end of the inside attic, which was nearly dark all over. It had lived there for years, because one of its white china ears was chipped, so that it was no longer a possible ornament for the spare bedroom.

Tavy found it at the end of a wicked and glorious afternoon. He had been left alone. The servants were the only other people in the house. He had promised to be good. He had meant to be good. And he had not been. The last thing he had done was to explore the attic, where he was never allowed to go, and to knock down the white cat from its shelf.

The sound of its fall brought the servants. The cat was not broken – only its other ear was chipped. Tavy was put to bed. But he got out as soon as the servants had gone downstairs, crept up to the attic, secured the cat, and washed it in the bath. So that when mother came back from London, Tavy, dancing impatiently at the head of the stairs, in a very wet nightgown, flung himself upon her and cried, "I've been awfully naughty, and I'm frightfully sorry, and please may I have the white cat for my very own?"

He was much sorrier than he had expected to be when he saw that mother was too tired even to want to know, as she generally did, exactly how naughty he had been. She only kissed him, and said, "I am sorry you've been naughty, my darling. Go back to bed now."

Tavy was ashamed to say anything more about the china cat, so he went back to bed. But he took the cat with him, and talked to it and kissed it, and went to sleep with its smooth shiny shoulder against his cheek.

In the days that followed, he was extravagantly good. Being good seemed as easy as being bad usually was. This may have been because mother seemed so tired and ill, and gentlemen in black coats and high hats came to see mother, and after they had gone she used to cry. These things going on in a house sometimes make people good, sometimes they act just the other way. Or it may have been because he had the china cat to talk to. Anyhow, whichever way it was, at the end of the week mother said, "Tavy, you've been a great comfort to me. You have tried very hard to be good."

It was difficult to say, "No, I haven't, at least not since the first day," but Tavy got it said, and was hugged for his pains.

"You wanted," said mother, "the china cat. Well, you may have it. But you must be very careful not to break it. And you mustn't give it away. It goes with the house. Your Aunt Jane made me promise to keep it in the family. It's very, very old. Don't take it out of doors for fear of accidents."

"I love the white cat, mother," said Tavy. "I love it better than all my toys."

Then mother told Tavy several things, and that night when he went to bed Tavy repeated them all faithfully to the china cat, who was about six inches high and looked very intelligent.

"So you see," he ended, "the wicked lawyer's taken nearly all mother's money, and we've got to leave our own lovely big white house, and go and live in a horrid little house. And mother does hate it so."

"I don't wonder," said the china cat very distinctly.

"What!" said Tavy, halfway into his nightshirt.

"I said, I don't wonder, Octavius," said the china cat, and rose from her sitting position, stretched her china legs and waved her white china tail.

"You can speak?" said Tavy.

"Can't you see I can? Hear I mean?" said the cat. "I belong to you now, so I can speak to you. I couldn't before. It wouldn't have been good manners."

Tavy, his nightshirt round his neck, sat down on the edge of the bed with his mouth open.

"Come, don't look so silly," said the cat, taking a walk along the high wooden mantelpiece, "anyone would think you didn't like me to talk to you."

"I'd love you to," said Tavy recovering himself a little.

"Well then," said the cat.

"May I touch you?" Tavy asked timidly.

"Of course! I belong to you. Look out!" The china cat gathered herself together and jumped. Tavy caught her.

It was quite a shock to find when one stroked her that the china cat, though alive, was still china, hard, cold, and smooth to the touch, and yet perfectly brisk and absolutely bendable as any flesh-and-blood cat.

"I wish you were a real cat," said Tavy.

"I am," said the cat. "Now how shall we amuse ourselves? I suppose you don't care for mousing?"

"I never tried," said Tavy, "and I think I rather wouldn't."

"Very well then, Octavius," said the cat. "I'll take you to the white cat's castle. Get into bed. Bed makes a good travelling carriage, especially when you haven't any other. Shut your eyes."

Tavy did as he was told. He shut his eyes, but could not keep them shut. He opened them a tiny, tiny chink, and sprang up. He was not in bed. He was on a couch of soft cloth, and the couch stood in a splendid hall, whose walls were of gold and ivory. By him stood the white cat, no longer china, but a real life cat with fur.

"Here we are," she said. "The journey didn't take

long, did it? Now we'll have that splendid supper, out of the fairytale, with the invisible hands waiting on us."

She clapped her paws – paws now as soft as white velvet – and a tablecloth floated into the room, then knives and forks and spoons and glasses, the table was laid, the dishes drifted in and they began to eat. There happened to be every single thing Tavy liked best to eat. After supper there was music and singing, and Tavy, having kissed a white, soft, furry forehead, went to bed in a gold four-poster with a counterpane of butterflies' wings. He awoke at home. On the mantelpiece sat the white cat, looking as though butter would not melt in her mouth. And all her furriness had gone with her voice. She was silent and china.

Tavy spoke to her. But she would not answer. Nor did she speak all day. Only at night when he was getting into bed she suddenly mewed and said, "Make haste, there's a play acted tonight at my castle."

Tavy made haste, and was rewarded by another glorious evening in the castle of the white cat.

And so the weeks went on. Days full of an ordinary little boy's joys and sorrows; nights spent by a little prince in the magic castle of the white cat.

Then came the day when Tavy's mother spoke to him, and he told the china cat what she had said.

"I knew this would happen," said the cat. "It always does. So you're to leave your house next week. Well, there's only one way out of the difficulty. Draw your sword, Tavy, and cut off my head and tail."

"And then will you turn into a princess, and shall I have to marry you?" Tavy asked with horror.

"No, dear – no," said the cat reassuringly. "I shan't turn into anything. But you and mother will turn into happy people. I shall just not be any more – for you."

"Then I won't do it," said Tavy.

"But you must. Come, draw your sword, like a brave fairy prince, and cut off my head."

The sword hung above his bed, with the helmet and breastplate Uncle James had given him last Christmas.

"I'm not a fairy prince," said the child. "I'm Tavy – and I love you."

"You love your mother better," said the cat. "Come cut my head off. The story always ends like that. You love mother best. It's for her sake."

"Yes." Tavy was trying to think it out. "Yes, I love mother best. But I won't cut off your head."

"Then," said the cat, "I must do what I can!"

She stood up, waving her white china tail, and before Tavy could stop her she had leapt, not, as before, into his arms, but onto the wide hearthstone.

It was all over – the china cat lay broken. The sound of the smash brought mother running.

"What is it?" she cried. "Oh, Tavy – the china cat!"

"She did it," sobbed Tavy. "She wanted me to cut off her head and I wouldn't."

"Don't talk nonsense, dear," said mother sadly. "That only makes it worse. Pick up the pieces."

"There's only two pieces," said Tavy. "Couldn't you stick her together again?"

"Why," said mother, holding the pieces close to the candle. "She's been broken before. And mended."

"I knew that," said Tavy, still sobbing. "Oh, my dear white cat!"

"Come, crying won't mend her," said mother. "Look, there's another piece, close to the shovel."

"That's not a piece of cat," he said, and picked it up.

It was a pale parchment label, tied to a key. Mother held it to the candle and read, "Key of the lock behind the knot in the mantelpiece panel in the white parlour."

"Tavy! I wonder! But where did it come from?"

"Out of my white cat, I suppose," said Tavy, his tears stopping. "Are you going to see what's in the mantelpiece panel,

Mother? Are you?"

They went downstairs to the white parlour. But they could not see any knot in the mantelpiece panel, because it was all painted white. But mother's fingers felt softly all over it, and found a round raised spot. It was a knot, sure enough. Then she scraped round it with her scissors, till she loosened the knot, and poked it out with the scissors point.

"I don't suppose there's any keyhole there really," she said. But there was. And what is more, the key fitted. The panel swung open, and inside was a little cupboard with two shelves. What was on the shelves? There were old laces and old embroideries, old jewellery and old silver, there was money, and there were dusty old papers that Tavy thought most uninteresting. But mother did not think them uninteresting. She laughed, and cried, or nearly cried, and said:

"Oh, Tavy, this was why the china cat was to be taken such care of!"

Then she told him how, one-hundred-and-fifty years before, the head of the house had gone out to fight for the pretender, and had told his daughter to take the greatest care of the china cat. "I will send you word of the reason by a sure hand," he said, for they parted on the open square, where any spy might have overheard anything. And he had been killed by an ambush not ten miles from home – and his daughter had never known. But she had kept the cat.

"And now it has saved us," said mother. "We can stay in the dear old house, and there are two other houses that will belong to us too, I think. And, oh, Tavy, would you like some pound cake and ginger wine, dear?"

Tavy did like. And had it.

The china cat was mended, but it was put in the glass-fronted corner cupboard in the drawing-room, because it had saved the house.

Now I dare say you'll think this is all nonsense, and a

made-up story. Not at all. If it
were, how would you account
for Tavy's finding,
the very next
night, fast asleep on
his pillow, his
own white cat –
the furry friend that the china cat used to turn into
every evening – the dear hostess who had amused him
so well in the white cat's fairy palace?

It was she, beyond a doubt, and that was why Tavy
didn't mind a bit about the china cat being taken from
him and kept under glass. You may think that it was
just any old stray white cat that had come in by
accident. Tavy knows better. It has the very same
tender tone in its purr that the magic white cat had. It
will not talk to Tavy, it is true, but Tavy can and does
talk to it. But the thing that makes it perfectly certain
that it is the white cat is that the tips of its two ears are
missing just as the china cat's ears were. If you say that
it might have lost its ear-tips in battle you are the kind
of person who always makes difficulties, and you may
be quite sure that the kind of splendid magics that
happened to Tavy will never happen to you.

The Nutcracker Prince

Retold from the original tale
by Ernst Hoffmann

DR DROSSELMEIER was an old man with a secret. In his youth, he had been the most nimble-fingered craftsman in the royal court.

Dr Drosselmeier had made clocks that were mechanical wonders. Some chimed with a hundred tinkling bells. Others were decorated with tiny musicians that danced and played their instruments as they struck the hour. Some even had secret doors, out of which little birds fluttered and flew around the room, chirruping the passing minutes. Yes, Dr Drosselmeier's clocks had been the talk of the palace. But the most amazing thing he had ever made was a mouse-trap.

Dr Drosselmeier had
invented a brilliant clockwork trap
that caught mice in their hundreds, twenty-
four hours a day. Everyone in the palace had been
delighted – except for the Mouse King. He too had
lived in the palace with his subjects. Now, he was
forced to leave and find another home, and he was
furious about it. The Mouse King knew powerful
magic and he took his revenge on Dr Drosselmeier by
turning his nephew into an ugly, wooden doll.

The doll wore a painted soldier's uniform and it had
a prince's crown painted mockingly onto its head, and
its jaws moved so it could crack nuts between its teeth.
The Mouse King's spell was so strong that there was
only one way to undo it. Firstly, the nutcracker prince
had somehow to kill the evil Mouse King. And
secondly, a little girl had to love him, in spite of his

ugliness. Well, Dr Drosselmeier had no idea where the Mouse King had gone, and he certainly didn't know a little girl kind enough to take pity on the poor, ugly wooden doll. And so his nephew had stayed a nutcracker.

From that moment on, Dr Drosselmeier had never made another clock. He lost all heart for mechanical things and so he lost his job at the palace, too. Dr Drosselmeier blamed himself entirely for his nephew's dreadful disappearance and he had never breathed a word of what had happened to anyone. But ever since, he had been trying to find a way to break the Mouse King's spell… and at last, he thought he had.

Dr Drosselmeier's goddaughter, Clara, had grown into the kindest little girl anyone could wish to meet. If any little girl was going to take pity on the stiff, glaring nutcracker prince, it would be Clara.

Now it was Christmas Eve, and Dr Drosselmeier had arrived at Clara's house trembling with excitement. He wasn't excited because there was a party going on with games and music and dancing. No, Dr Drosselmeier was excited because tonight was the night he hoped the evil magic would be undone and his nephew would return to life.

While the party guests talked and joked and laughed

together, Dr Drosselmeier set about emptying the huge bag he had brought with him. It was filled with gingerbread and shortcake, candy walking sticks and sugar pigs, nuts and bon bons, nougat and humbugs... High and low, in every corner of the room, Dr Drosselmeier heaped piles of all the Mouse King's favourite things to eat. That should tempt him out from wherever he's hiding, thought Dr Drosselmeier, determinedly.

Then it was time to give Clara her Christmas present. The little girl's eyes opened wide with excitement as she stripped off the sparkly paper. But her face suddenly fell as she saw the ugly nutcracker prince. Then, gently, Clara stroked the doll's face. He wasn't cute, he wasn't cuddly – he wasn't even new! But that was exactly why Clara decided she loved him. She couldn't bear to think of leaving him all alone, laughed at and unloved – especially at Christmas time. Clara clutched the nutcracker prince close to her and hugged him tight. And Dr Drosselmeier slipped away from the party, his heart light with hope...

When the party was over and it was bedtime at last, Clara tucked the wooden doll up next to her. "I love you," she whispered, just before she fell asleep. "I'll look after you always." And that night, Clara had a very strange dream. She dreamt that the nutcracker prince woke up beside her. He smiled at Clara and held her hand, and led her downstairs. There was scuffling and squeaking coming from the drawing room, and when Clara peeped around the door she saw a terrible sight. There were mice everywhere! They were climbing all over Dr Drosselmeier's goodies, fighting and biting to get at the sweets. And worst of all, a horrible seven-headed mouse was standing in the middle of the carpet, cackling with glee at all the arguing and the mess. The seven-headed mouse wore seven gold crowns and Clara could tell he must be the king of the evil creatures.

Very bravely, the nutcracker prince charged at the gruesome Mouse King with a sword glinting in his hand and began to fight furiously. But he was completely outnumbered. The mice swarmed to their king's defence. They dragged the nutcracker prince to the ground and he disappeared under a thousand biting, clawing bodies. Just as the Mouse King threw back his head and began to laugh, Clara tore her slipper off her foot and threw it at him with all her might. WHAM! It hit the Mouse King on four of his seven horrible heads. He staggered to and fro for a second, and then collapsed dead to the floor.

As soon as the mice saw that their leader was no more, their courage deserted them. They hurried to scoop up his body and then they were gone, streaming off through cracks in the wall, holes in the skirting and gaps in the floorboards.

The nutcracker prince ran to Clara and kissed her. "Thank you for all you have done for me," he whispered, and there were tears sparkling in his painted eyes. "Let me repay you by taking you on a wonderful journey to my kingdom, the realm of sweets…"

It was the most wonderful dream Clara had ever had. She travelled through forests made of barley sugar, crossed rivers that ran with lemonade, picked flowers of sherbert, walked on paths of chocolate, and visited the nutcracker prince's gingerbread castle. In fact, Clara was very sorry to be woken up – even though it was Christmas Day itself! She hugged the wooden doll and told him, "You're the best present I've ever had," and she could have sworn that his smile was even broader than usual.

Meanwhile, across the city, Dr Drosselmeier had also woken up to find the best present he'd ever had. There sprawled underneath his Christmas tree, sleeping an exhausted but peaceful sleep, was his brave, handsome nephew...

Sleeping Beauty

Retold from the original tale
by Charles Perrault

LONG, *LONG* ago, when fairies were still able to grant wishes, there lived a king and queen who wanted, more than anything in the whole world, to have a baby daughter. When their wish was finally granted and a beautiful tiny princess lay in her cradle, the king and queen decided to have a great candlelit party to celebrate.

They invited the twelve most important fairies in the land and a great many other people besides.

As well as the thousands of glittering candles, there were golden tables piled high with all kinds of delicious food, and the royal orchestra played their most cheerful tunes. The twelve fairies all lined up to present their christening gifts to the tiny princess. Their gifts were those that only a fairy can give: beauty, kindness, grace, honesty and the like. The princess smiled happily in her cradle as one by one the fairies tiptoed up.

The eleventh fairy had just promised the princess a sweet singing voice, when there was a great roll of thunder and all the candles flickered out. There stood quite the most wicked fairy anyone had ever seen. She was dressed all in black, her long straggly hair was black and her eyes, glittering in rage, were as black as the crow's feathers. Her voice was like a saw as she screeched, "How dare you not invite me to the party! I too have a gift for the little princess," and she smiled a not very nice smile. "Because you have forgotten me, my gift is that when the princess is sixteen she shall prick her finger on a spindle and die!" and with a horrid laugh, the wicked fairy disappeared.

As the candles were hastily relit, everyone started talking at once. Then a quiet voice was heard over all hubbub. It was the twelfth fairy.

"I cannot undo this wicked spell," she whispered, "but I can decree that the princess will not die. She will instead fall into a deep sleep for a hundred years," and all the fairies slipped away leaving the court in despair.

The king, of course, immediately ordered that all the spinning wheels in the land were to be burned. After a while, everyone grew less frightened, and as the princess grew up into the most lovely girl, the wicked fairy's prediction slipped from most people's memories.

On her sixteenth birthday the princess went exploring. At the top of a tower she did not remember seeing before, she found an old woman, sitting at a spinning wheel.It was, of course, the wicked fairy in disguise. The princess was fascinated and, as she bent forward to look at the cloth, her hand caught the sharp spindle and she immediately fell to the ground as though dead. With a swirl of smoke and a nasty laugh, the wicked fairy disappeared.

Everyone else in the palace fell asleep at the same moment. The king fell asleep with his ministers, the queen and her maids fell asleep in her dressing room. The cook fell asleep in the kitchen in the middle of baking a cake, the groom fell asleep as he fed the horses in the stables and even the little linnet the princess had in a golden cage by her bedside fell asleep on its perch. A great high thorn hedge grew up and soon the palace was completely hidden. Time stood still and all was silent.

Many, many years passed. The tale of the sleeping princess spread far and wide, and many came to try to find her. But no one could get through the thorn hedge. And so after even more years, people forgot what lay behindthe hedge.

Then one day a handsome prince came riding through the woods. As he reached the thorn hedge, thousands of pink roses burst into bloom and a path appeared, leading through the hedge towards the palace. It was a hundred years to the day since the princess had pricked her finger. The prince was astonished by the sight that met his eyes. Everywhere people lay asleep, frozen in the midst of whatever they had been doing when the spell caught them.

The prince climbed the tower, and there he found the princess, looking as lovely as ever. He bent over and kissed her, and immediately the spell was broken. The king and his ministers carried on just where they had left off. The queen chose which dress she wanted to wear and the maids brushed her hair. The cook put her cake in the oven and the groom led the horses out into the courtyard. And even the little linnet in her golden cage sang a joyful song.

As for the princess...
Well, she and the prince
had fallen in love
with each other on
the spot, and were
married the very
next day. They all
lived happily ever
after, and the wicked
fairy was never
ever seen again.